T0209844

Heart OF A Servant Royally Positioned

TRESIA A.D. DANIEL

WESTBOW
PRESS®
A DIVISION OF THOMAS NELSON
& ZONDERVAN

WestBow Press books may be ordered through booksellers or by contacting:

WestBow Press
A Division of Thomas Nelson & Zondervan
1663 Liberty Drive
Bloomington, IN 47403
www.westbowpress.com
1 (866) 928-1240

ISBN: 978-1-9736-5064-5 (sc)
ISBN: 978-1-9736-5063-8 (e)

Print information available on the last page.

WestBow Press rev. date: 03/26/2019

DEDICATION

This devotional book is dedicated to God who has blessed me with the ability and every good gift. My husband Rev. H. Ron Daniel II who believed in me to see this process through to the end. My children Rondré, Tréon and Rozèn Daniel and my parents Anthony & Violet Nisbett & Hastings & Mova Daniel for all of their love and support. To my wonderful sister Tamicia Lestrade thank you for the vote of confidence.

FOREWORD

To become royally positioned one must humble themselves under the mighty hand of God. There are many persons who would have missed out on their promise because of their abject refusal to humble themselves. The Bible tells us in James 4:6 that God resists the proud and gives grace to the humble. Matthew 20:26 tells us that whoever wants to be great must become a servant and in Mark 10:45 tells us that our savior came to serve, not be served. In this our generation many persons are looking for fame to be noticed and positions of honour or authority. In order to rise to the promises, one must first become a servant. Not too many of us like serving as much as we like to be served. Through this devotional it is my hope that the readers will find areas of their lives that need to be surrendered and come down from their lofty place so that God will be allowed to elevate them to the royal positions that he has for them. After all we are the King's kid so royal blood already runs through our veins; we just have to go through the process so that we can have the keys to operate in our positions.

Repentance

A servant must know who his/her master is. Repentance reestablishes this relationship that has been distorted by sin. The next few pages of devotionals will take us through the journey of repentance.

If my people, who are called by my name, will humble themselves and pray and seek my face and turn from their wicked ways, then I will hear from heaven, and I will forgive their sin and will heal their land.

2 Chronicles 7:14

DAY 1

When God is mad at you...................

Key Verse: 2 Chronicles 34:19-33

Whenever our loved ones are mad at us, we bend our back to ensure that we return to their good graces. Any angry wife may receive fresh flowers, folded laundry or even a box of chocolate as an act of repentance. Children may complete their chores without being asked. Sometimes however, the wrong gift is brought and the tension continues for prolonged periods.

When the Lord identifies issues in our lives, our home, our church our country, he expects one thing REPENTANCE. Repentance places things in the correct perspective. God is once again returned to his rightful place as master, ruler, king and we become servants royally positioned.

Just like our parents, God gets mad to signal there is a matter that needs to be addressed. God gets mad to get our attention. God gets mad to propel us into action. God gets mad to aid us in avoiding punishment. Josiah understood the purpose of God's anger and as a result, he sprang into action.

Have you been hearing the Lord speak time and time again concerning you? Is his still small voice now a roar? It is very possible God is mad at you. He is calling for repentance as this is the only gift that will work. Follow Josiah's lead enquire of the master and REPENT!

Prayer: Father You know the depths of my heart, search me now o God. See if there be some wicked way in me and purify me

DAY 2

Come back to me, but it's your choice.....................

Key Verse: Joel 2:1-12

I'm coming back to the heart of worship and it's all about you…... I stood at the altar one Sunday as we repeated the line "Lord it's all about you" God was saying to me "Is it really all about me? It seems to be all about you."

Many times we sing lies maybe because the beats are good or the songs are catchy but as the Lord blindsided me that morning I ask you, is it really all about God? If you paused the answer is probably NO. If you are always really busy it is NO, if you are filled with excuses it's a NO. Selfishness is innate in all of us but as we veer off course God often times has to jolt us back to his direction. The prophet Joel explained to the Israelites that God's judgement was pending and he outlined in great details the judgement of the Lord. Repentance came down to a choice. They changed the pending judgement of God by choosing repentance. God forces himself on no one. Repentance is choosing God's way in word thought and deed. It is denying my way and Satan's way for God's way. Back to the heart of worship? There is no other way but it is your choice.

Prayer: Father I am thankful that You have given to every man the freedom of choice. Today I thank You for that choice and I choose to return to the heart of worship where it is all about You.

DAY 3

An "I'm Sorry" from the heart..................

Key Verse: Joel 2:13

My niece and nephew were spending their Easter with our family and an issue occurred between my niece and my son that required an apology. The responses were varied but the Lord used this experience to teach me a valuable lesson. One cried before apologizing and it took a while for the words to come, the other apologized and then burst into tears. When I asked why are you crying? My son replied "I do not like saying sorry it makes me feel bad."

There are so many of us like these children in our Christian walk. Apologizing for our actions? "What is that?" Instead, we find creative ways to explain or justify our actions or we simply do not acknowledge the wrong and move on like nothing happened.

In Joel 2:12-13 the Lord was saying to Israel he was not impressed with outward acts and wanted an "I'm sorry" from the heart. The kind of apology that causes one to see where we are and where God is. The kind of "I'm sorry" that drives us to tears when we realize the error of our ways and when we realize how we have disappointed God. The kind of "I'm sorry" that forces us to change, to be different. Today we acknowledge our wrongs and seek the father's forgiveness. Just like the children of Israel the Lord is awaiting an "I'm sorry" from the heart. True Repentance!!

Prayer: Father You have searched me and have identified some wicked way in me. Father today I repent out of a sincere heart. Out of a heart that is broken because of the current state. Father I ask Your forgiveness today.

DAY 4

I've outgrown this place.....

Key Verse: Genesis 26:1-16

So many of us love "the comfortable". It is the place we have grown accustomed to, the place we grew and accomplished and for most of us we settle in this place. We know how things work here in the comfortable and we know the people in the comfortable. We know who is for us and who is against us in the comfortable. In the comfortable we are familiar with our surroundings. However, there comes a time when the Lord is ready to enlarge our coast and increase our borders. We also know when we get to that place but our hearts long for the comfortable. While our hearts yearn, God is saying you have outgrown this place. We know we have outgrown this place when the very people who invited us in wants us out, it is time move on less you become God of your domain. When you are no longer impacted by what or who is around you and the growing ceases, it is time to depart the comfortable.

Oh, but our hearts long to hold on to what is comfortable but this prevents us from getting what God has for us. Moving forward means forgetting what is behind and pressing towards the mark of the higher calling. What is God calling you from? Is it a job a relationship? Is it a way of thinking? Stop procrastinating and start walking! You have outgrown this place, your future is calling!

Prayer—Father You know the fears in my heart for the unknown. Lord quiet the storms in my mind and heart that tries to bully me into staying in the comfortable. I want to fulfil my destiny please help me to do so. In Jesus Name Amen.

DAY 5

The Price of Surrender

Key Verse: Luke 22:42

What am I willing to give up? When I sing "I surrender all" do I really mean "all" or should I be singing I surrender "some"? Am I really willing to sacrifice what I want for what God says? Am I really willing to give up what I want? What does a surrendered life look like? Jesus said "not my will but thine". In other words Jesus was saying, "Dad I don't want to do this crucifixion thing but not my will." You may be saying, "I feel like giving up but not my will." "I like it here God but not my will." "I am tired of giving up friends but not my will" "I cannot take another rejection but Lord not my will" "This one is hard Lord but not my will." "I surrender" means I am completely sold out to God. "I surrender" means I am walking in complete obedience. "I surrender" means I am willing to step out of my comfort zone to the place of the unknown to me, but known to God. "I surrender" means it does not matter what I want but what God wants always supersedes my wants or desires. "I surrender" means not my will, but God's!

Prayer—Lord often times my desires clash with Yours. Help me to walk in humility so that I can put Your will above my own always. In Jesus name Amen

DAY 6

Repentance Restores

Key Verse: Joel 2:25

Joel Chapter 1 tells us what the palmer worm didn't eat the locust ate and what the locust didn't eat the cankerworm ate and what the cankerworm didn't eat the caterpillar ate. This speaks to total destruction. Often times we go through seasons where it looks like total devastation. Physically and spiritually we are dry, broken and dead. It seems as though we cannot get a break no matter where we turn. Today I am thankful for the promise that is in Joel Chapter 2:25 that speaks to restoration. The return of all that was taken, Praise God! God's heart was turned to his people because they came before him broken. The priests came off their lofty place and was broken for themselves and the people. The people also became broken for themselves. God's pity is provoked by true repentance; the kind of repentance that is voluntary and comes straight from the heart. The kind of repentance that comes from an admittedly broken place. No FAÇADE, NO MASKS!! When we get to the place where we see ourselves in the light of the word, NO PRETENSE then the weight of the word can break us and evoke true repentance. The kind of repentance that restores.

Prayer: Father I am thankful that You forgive and I can come boldly to Your throne. Today I ask for Your restoration. Father restore the joy of my salvation, restore my peace and restore everything the enemy has stolen. In Jesus Name Amen

Moving Forward

So you have repented now what? Well on this journey after repentance we are expected to grow and glow. The next few pages will take you through a few spiritual truths that will make the difference between whether you stand or fall. Join me it's time to move forward.

For I know the plans I have for you," declares the LORD, "plans to prosper you and not to harm you, plans to give you hope and a future. Jeremiah 29:11 NIV

DAY 7

Hold on to what you know

Key Verse: 2 Kings 2:17

Elisha had just experienced one of the greatest miracles which was foretold by Elijah. With this miracle he was in line to receive the blessing of a double portion. However, when he returned to civilization people tried to convince him that his experience was fake and Elisha caved in to peer pressure robbing him the joys of the most exciting time in his life. I began sharing my faith journey with a young lady as it relates to the provision of God during the building of our home. She couldn't understand the whole God thing or the faith thing. In the process of our conversation, she tried to convince me that all that occurred was luck or coincidence. There are many persons who will try to talk you out of your "God experience" because it makes them uncomfortable, it makes them jealous or they are trying to disqualify your anointing.

Like Elisha, they try to convince us that it never happened. The truth is an experience is personal. Let no man talk you out of what you have experienced. Hold on to what you know and what glory has been revealed. No one but you knows the level of investment you have made in the kingdom and no one but you know what God has done. Let no man deceive or distract you hold on to what you know and what you have experienced.

Prayer—Father help us to not allow the thoughts of others to influence Your work in our lives. Help us to hold on to what we know in You. Help us to trust what heaven says over the multitude of men. In Jesus name Amen

DAY 8

Fix your eyes

Key Verse: 2 Corinthians 6:18

It is so amazing how our attention is so easily taken whether by a loud noise, people passing, an accident or a strange outfit. We get hung up on the behaviours and attitudes of others and we become distracted. We are reminded to not look at what we can see but what cannot be seen. We see with our eyes a mountain of debt but with our faith we see provision. We see sickness with our eyes but health with our faith. We see trouble with our eyes but peace with our faith. So where are you looking? Are you looking at what your eyes can see or what your faith can achieve if you will simply believe? It is easy to have our faith blinded by the things we see with our natural eyes. I encourage us today to close our physical eyes and open our eyes of faith. Once you do that, keep your eyes fixed on the God that can part waters, rain food from heaven, spring water from a rock and turn water into wine. Fix your eyes on God!!!

Prayer—Lord I am tempted to look around when the cares of life becomes overwhelming. Help me to keep my eyes on You and above my problems. In Jesus name Amen

DAY 9

Too Quick to Forget

Key Verse: Hebrews 13:8

There is a popular song I heard growing up that had the words "what have you done for me lately?" It is funny how sometimes as Christians we are easy to forget. We forget past blessings but keep past struggles at the forefront. We forget that our God does not change. We forget that he is the same yesterday today and forever. We forget that God is not like man and he will not lie. It doesn't matter what is going on today and it doesn't change who he was, is or will be to us. God is reliable! We can count on him to perform consistently well. Don't forget past triumphs as they help to keep in focus the nature of our daddy who we can trust. When he doesn't give the answer you wanted for the prayer today, remember who he was yesterday and that same God is who he is today. Even if God has not done anything for you lately and that's a lie, He is still the same.

Prayer : Father help me to trust Your heart and Your words. Help me to trust that You mean what You say and you say what you mean. Help me to know and believe that You are reliable. In Jesus name Amen.

COMMITMENT

Trust

Every good relationship is built on the fundamental principle of trust. The same applies to our God relationship. We really cannot move forward with God unless we trust him. Until we have that firm belief in the reliability, truth or ability of God, moving forward is impossible. In the next few pages we will explore Trusting God.......

"where He leads me I will follow...I'll go with him all the way."

-Ernest W Blandy 1890

DAY 10

God is my refuge... Really?

Key Verse Psalm 91:1

God you are my shelter from pursuit, danger or trouble. God I have a firm belief in the reliability of your truth, your ability and your strength. In you God, I am protected from danger and I will not be harmed. There are so many things chasing us; people, their thoughts and my thoughts, problems whether financial, physical or emotional. We seem to always be chased by the enemy who is in pursuit of our souls. The truth is, I know that God is my shelter from the storms of life and I know that in him, I am safe. However, to know and to believe are two completely different things. You can know something yet don't believe. To know and believe, comes down to a matter of trust. Do you trust God or do you think you trust God? For a long time I knew that God was and is my refuge but I didn't always believe. How do I know this? I always had a backup plan. Somewhere deep in my heart I didn't believe that the eternal God was my refuge. I was always waiting for him to disappoint so I couldn't trust fully. What is your hindrance to blind faith or total trust? What is that one thing that stands between you and complete trust in the almighty God? Today may you name it and shame it so that God can truly be your refuge.

Prayer—Lord I know that You are my refuge, I know that You will shelter me and protect me. Father help my heart and soul to believe what my mind already knows in Jesus Name Amen.

DAY 11

Trust the Shepherd

Key Verse: Psalm 23:1

David had a pretty good understanding of where he stood. He knew that the Almighty God, Alpha and Omega, Jehovah Jireh, Rapha, Shalom, Sabaoth, Nissi et al the Everlasting Father, the I am God was his Lord and his Shepherd. He knew who his Shepherd was and knew enough to be in a relationship with such a Shepherd. He also knew by virtue of being in this divine relationship his needs would be met. Why then do we worry? Do we know who our shepherd is? Is our shepherd the Lord or are our plans and hard work our shepherd? If we really knew our shepherd, we would know with a complete assurance that we would not want. Circumstances of life has taught us not to trust but today I challenge us to get to know who we are trusting. We can trust the Lord who knows when to lead and when to guide, when to provide and when to comfort. Our God promises never to leave us nor forsake us!! May we trust him today!

Prayer: Father today I confess that I have not always trusted the plan of the good Shepherd. I confess that I have had plans that I felt were better than Your thoughts towards me. Today Lord I ask You to help my unbelief and to trust that the good shepherd, which is who You are will look after me. In Jesus name amen.

DAY 12

Who He was is who He will always be

Key Verse: Hebrews 13:8

Over the course of my life I have experienced many yesterdays. As I reflected on this passage I was forced to recall who God was in my yesterday. In my yesterday, God was a healer when he healed my eyesight from near blindness, high blood pressure from eclampsia and my liver that was affected by what only God knows. He was and still is provider even more so during my three year stint of unemployment. I chose the major blessings to share with you but God has done countless things in my yesterday. If God did it before in my yesterday I am assured that he can do it again in my today and forever. Whatever our today holds, we can hold on to God's word that who he was in our yesterday situation is who he will be today and forever.

Prayer: Father God today I thank you that You are a God that changes not. I thank You that I can use yesterday as an indication of what my tomorrow with you will be like. Faithful You have been Lord and faithful you will always be. Thank You for being that constant in my life when so many things are prone to change. In Jesus name, amen.

DAY 13

Is Your Heart Set to God?

Key Verse: Colossians 3:1

Whenever things happen in our lives it makes us shift our focus from God, to whatever is going on around us. Today I ask the question, what is your heart set on? We are reminded to keep our hearts on God no matter the circumstances. Even if the bank didn't give the response you hoped for; set your heart on God. Even if the doctor's report isn't exactly what you hoped for; set your heart on God. Maybe you hoped that a situation at work would have been handled differently; set your heart on God. Maybe your spouse disappointed you based on some action or inaction; set your heart on God. Set suggests some deliberate action on our part. It is a conscious decision to maintain our God focus no matter what. Some may say that you are a little silly and you are a little stupid to have this much confidence in a God that you cannot see. I hasten to remind you that this God was here long before us and will be here long after so He has a good track record. No matter what life throws your way today set your heart in God's direction.

Prayer: Father today I confess that I have not always set my heart towards heaven. Often times I am distracted by the cares of life and circumstances around me. Lord today I ask that you will keep me looking up so that You can guide and direct my life in Jesus name Amen.

DAY 14

Stir it up!

Key Verse: Hebrews 13:8

As Paul laid wait for his execution in the cold dark cell he wrote to his spiritual son sharing many things; one of which was "how to manoeuvre spiritual hardships". Paul reminded him that his gift of faith came down his bloodline and he was convinced Timothy had it too. His gift just needed stirring up. Often times when we go through hardships we forget who we are and whose we are. Sometimes we feel alone and forgotten by the very God we are here to serve. Timothy lived in an age where Christians were tortured and killed and I can perfectly understand if his heart became weak and he began to fear at the realization that his mentor was about to be killed. It is amidst this chaotic scene that Paul reminds Timothy that fear is not of God! Fear is the counterfeit, Faith is the gift. Today there may be some situation in your life that is causing you to fear. You may be afraid of the future, death, lack of finances, rejection, being alone or being unloved. You may fear that God will not provide, he will not heal or strengthen. Maybe you fear that he will not come through this time. Today I encourage us to stir up faith. Start fanning the flames again through prayer and reading the word and meditating on the right things. Your granny had it, your mother had and I know it is in you so stir it up!

Prayer: Father God today I thank you that You are a God that can help my unbelief. Today Lord I ask you to grant the strength I need to stir up faith in my heart so that I can fully trust and believe in You. I admit that my faith has wavered but today I recommit to stirring it up and into action in Jesus name Amen.

COMMITMENT

God's Love

Until we come in contact with God's love, we cannot love others the way the creator intended. True love comes from God. Contact must be made with the divine love source before it can be extended to others.

"The love of God how rich and pure how measureless and strong it shall forevermore endure the saints and angels song."

-Frederick M Lehman 1917

DAY 15

Jesus Loved me enough to die...........

Key Verse: Joel 3:16

Would you die for someone you didn't know? Would you make a purposeful decision to pay a debt you didn't owe? What if you could see the future and realize these same persons would deny you, lie on you, turn their backs on you, reject your sacrifice and ultimately reject your love; would you chose to die? Knowing all that he knew, Jesus chose to die for us. He took on all of our sins suffered and died for us. The king of kings stepped off of his throne suffered and died for us. He didn't change his mind after he saw our hearts, our devious nature, self-centred ways, our anger and bitterness, our hatred, and jealousy, our lust, our pride. Oh pride, that same pride that causes us to deny him. God saw the depths of our hearts and loved us enough to die for us. Today Jesus wants us to accept this love. The kind of love that chose to die for us. Undeserving as we may be he chose to die. He has offered this love; accept it!! He loves us yes he does, he gave his life to prove it.

Prayer: Our Father and God thank you for dying on the cross for my sins, thank you for loving me that much. Thank You that even though I didn't deserve Your love, you gave it anyway. Thank you that through Your sacrifice I can have life more abundantly. In Jesus name Amen.

DAY 16

What are you afraid of?

Key Verse: 1 John 4:18

Are you afraid of the dark? Are you afraid of being hurt? Are you afraid of dying? Are you afraid people won't like you? Are you afraid of being alone? Are you afraid of stepping out? Are you afraid of public opinion? Are you afraid of failing? Are you always afraid?

God's love is perfectly free from fear, fault or defect. His love is complete, sacrificial and pure. His love comes with NO conditions and NO strings attached. His love is the purest love one could ever find. Many persons have not had the opportunity to experience this type of love from anyone on earth and this lack of love creates room for fear. Our experiences have taught us that this type of love is non-existent and the thought that a God I cannot see can offer this love is unbelievable. Yet our invisible God is always present even in times of trouble. His love manifests itself daily and it is perfect.

Until we embrace his love, fear will continue to abide in our hearts. Give fear its eviction notice today and invite love to come in and dwell with you.

Prayer: Dear Heavenly Father, I thank You that my human experiences do not define Your love. Father, today I ask You to cast out all fear from my heart: fear of failure, fear of death, fear of being hurt in any way. Father replace all fear with Your perfect love in Jesus name Amen.

DAY 17

Strength to believe..................

Key Verse: Ephesians 3: 16-18

Can this heart take another heart break? Can I endure any more pain? For most of us the answer is a resounding NO. So we resolve never to love again. While this option seemingly protects our hearts it keeps out the love of a lifetime – the love that Jehovah God offers us.

The Apostle Paul was very aware that some people cannot understand Jehovah's love. Some persons because of past experiences cannot accept that this kind of love exists. Paul in his writing is hopeful that we would have the strength to accept God's love; a love that covers our past, our present and our future. We cannot go above His love no matter how high life takes us nor are we ever beneath His love no matter how far we fall into sin. God's love covers us. Only the persons who have the strength to love one more time and be loved will experience God's love. May God strengthen our capacity to accept his love. To accept Jesus is to accept love as God is love.

Prayer: Our father and God, today I ask for strength. Strength to believe that a God like You can love someone like me. Strength to open my heart to the love of a Saviour after all of life's hurt. Strength to receive Your love so that I can give Your love to others. Father help my unbelief today and open my heart to love in Jesus' name Amen.

DAY 18

Loved Past my experiences.............

Key Verse: Ephesians 3:16-19

If you stood up in the rain without an umbrella you would expect to get wet. If you touched a hot stove you would expect to get burned. Our past experiences help to shape our future responses.

There are many persons who did not have a good family life growing up. The actions or inactions of their parents, friends, and family provided a very negative love base. Some persons were abandoned and taught that love abandons; some persons were abused and in essence were taught love hurts; and some persons were severely disappointed and were taught not to trust love as love disappoints.

Whatever our reality, God wants to move us past our experiences and allow Him to fill our hearts with His kind of love. To know God is to know true love. The problem for many of us is that we have known pain and heartache for so long that love becomes a suspect. That is why Paul wrote in earlier verses that he prayed that God would strengthen us so that we are in a position to accept God whose very nature is love.

The Apostle asked God to give us the strength to discard the negative ideas that shaped our love experiences and embrace the love experience of God. May the God of love uproot, bypass, rearrange or even demolish our ideas of what love is and cause us to be grounded in Him where we can find true love.

Prayer: Dear Heavenly Father my past experiences have taught me to guard my heart. In many ways I have even guarded it from You. Today Lord, in reckless abandon I give You my heart. I release all pain and all hurt of the past and I receive Your love today. In Jesus Name Amen.

DAY 19

Does all of me love God?........

Key Verse: Luke 10:27-28

We are often taught as children to leave room for disappointment. Our parents would have taught us this in an effort to protect our hearts from hurt. Strangely enough this very loving gesture on the part of our parents can have damaging effects on our spiritual walk.

Many of us do not love the Lord with everything. We are often waiting for Him to disappoint as we have been conditioned to believe or expect. So, if God's answer is delayed we are ready to give up. If it appears our petition is denied we feel betrayed. God wants us to love Him with ALL of our hearts, the seat of our thoughts. He wants us to love Him with all of our soul - that spirit man - because that's the only way we can commune with Him spirit to spirit.

Our actions must say we love God and that we understand that we are loved by Him. Our mind or conscience must love God in order for us to say and do the right things. What we feed our heart will guide our spirit, soul and actions towards our lover or away from Him. Our God gave all of Himself for us and in return He expects us to give all of ourselves and our love to Him. Does all of you love God or are you leaving room for disappointment?

Prayer: Father God, I thank you for the agape, sacrificial love that you have for me. Father, I thank You for loving me even when I don't deserve it. Father, forgive me for not accepting Your love in its entirety or returning my love in its entirety to You. Father, help me to love You and be loved by You totally. In Jesus name amen.

DAY 20

Where are you looking?

Key Verse: Psalm 73:1-3 (MSG)

Some persons will see the glass half full but if you are like me you tend to see the glass half empty. Where you are looking is determined by how you are looking and through whose eyes you are looking.

Many of us are holding God hostage for the 20% of prayers he has appeared to not answer, hasn't answered yet, or said wait. I have been guilty - like Asaph - of throwing a tantrum, becoming depressed, bitter or even envious of those who seem to be in a better position than me. Like Asaph, I almost missed God. I was so caught up in my unhappiness over my lost 20% that I almost missed all of the amazing 80% good he had done and was doing in my life.

What is that 20% that threatens to have you let go of all that God has done to become bitter and angry? Maybe you are not angry but you are sad and depressed or maybe you are jealous of those who have what you long for. Don't allow the enemy to cause you to look at the mole hill 20%. Instead, why don't you look at the 80% mountain of good God has done for you today?

I encourage all of us to change where we are looking lest our downcast souls cause us to miss God.

Prayer: Father God, today I ask Your forgiveness for thinking that my tantrums will move You. Father, forgive me for thinking pouting will change Your position. Father, today cause me to look at You. Keep my eyes focused on you and allow me to see my life through Your eyes. In Jesus name.

Deliverance

But I have prayed for thee, that thy faith fail not: and when thou art converted, strengthen thy brethren. Luke 22:32 KJV

"Jesus is a deliverer. I know He delivered me."

DAY 21

God's got you!

Key Verse Deuteronomy 33:27

Have you ever felt alone or like there was no one to depend on? Have you ever felt like everything you touched crumbled? Have you ever felt helpless or hopeless?

There was a time when I felt as though I was under a cloud of despair. During that period, I received a love letter from my Daddy

In that letter my Daddy reminded me that He has 'got me.' He is sheltering me from the storms because He is my refuge and under me His arms are there to carry me when I can't go on. He reminded me that He is there to pick me up when I fall, to wipe my tears, to comfort my heart and to hold me up from day to day. Finally and most importantly, He reminded me that He is there to guard my heart.

God had to remind me that 'He got me'. Before anything was He was and long after everything is gone He will still be. I encourage you to believe today that 'God got you.' Once you are walking with Him and even if you feel as though He is not walking with you just know He's 'got you'.

God promises never to leave us nor forsake us so may He help us to know that He will always be there.

Prayer: Father God, I thank you that you will never leave me nor forsake me and that even when I think all hope is gone You are always there. Thank You for the peace that can only come from You and knowing that You've got me in the palm of your hands. In Jesus name.

DAY 22

Changing My Outlook

Key Verse: James 1:2

Consider it pure joy whenever you face trials of many kinds ... What? Consider it joy?

When I read this, I thought James must have been crazy when he penned those words. I wondered if James ever lost a job. I wondered if James ever encountered an illness for which doctors had no cure. I wondered if James ever had any financial issues or had bill collectors hound him. I wondered when James wrote this what was he thinking?

As I read and reread this passage, I felt the Lord saying to me that James was in his right mind because the test or the trial is the beginning not the end. God has entrusted me with the test because He thinks I am able to pass it. The least I can do in return is to trust Him. When I am looking for answers I should look to Him and quit looking for the next answer that may only provide temporary relief or another disappointment.

Finally, if I embrace His will whole heartedly, I can count it joy because I know every situation is working for my good.

Today may we ask for grace to change our outlook so that instead of seeing storm clouds, we see rain clouds that will blow over.

Prayer: Father God, today I ask your forgiveness for looking at the storm instead of looking at the One who the wind and waves obey. Help me Lord to change my outlook and trust You the God that makes a way for us. In Jesus name

DAY 23

There are no shortcuts

Key Verse: James1:2

I love shortcuts.

I can usually find an easier way to do just about anything. I sit and analyse how to make things less stressful, easier. The funny thing is what we do in the natural we assume will work in the Spiritual but what I have realized is that there are no short cuts with God. The only way to produce perseverance is through trials. I searched and searched for another way but all scripture points to trials, suffering, and tribulation as the way to perseverance.

So there really isn't an easier way to access God's glory? There isn't an easier way to grow my faith? There really aren't any shortcuts to God's promises? Since the answer to all of the above is a resounding NO, I pray that God will grant us grace for the journey and strength for the battles. There is only one way to the promise. It is through the process. Quit looking for a way around the process and trust the guide.

Prayer: Father God, I thank you that you are patient with people like me who like things easy and often resist the hard things that you allow our way. Lord help us to be patient in trials. Help us to persevere so that we will be complete, lacking nothing. In Jesus name.

DAY 24

Tell Yourself the Truth

Key Verse 1 Samuel 15:17 (NIV)

How do you see yourself? Have you been lying to yourself trying to convince yourself you are something that you are not? Have you been trying to convince yourself that the thing that makes you who you are is not sin? Have you been able to admit to yourself that you are not perfect? Do you take mites out of the eyes of others while carrying a plank in yours? Do you tell yourself what sounds good, what you hope to be true one day but what isn't right now?

We often lie to ourselves to soften the impact. However, if God is going to be able to help us we have to be honest with ourselves. God will not fix what we won't admit. Have you been sugar coating stubbornness? God says stubbornness is idolatry. Maybe you are just a little doubtful but unbelief is sin. Are you a little fearful? Well fear is the absence of faith. Have you been walking in pride? God resists the proud and walks with the humble. Sometimes our truths sound so bad and as a result we are tempted to keep them hidden. However, whatever your truth be honest with yourself so that you can be better, grow and access the promises of God.

Prayer: Lord, it is often difficult to admit to myself and others the things that are wrong with me. I often pretend they do not exist for as long as I can. However, I know that You will not fix what I won't admit so I ask You to strengthen me to face the person I really am so that You can make me the person You want me to be in Jesus name.

DAY 25

Am I Deceiving myself

Key Verse: James 1:22

I had this dress that I loved. I also gained some weight that I didn't want to admit to myself. As I tried to squeeze into this dress one Sunday convincing myself it looked great my aunt, who was visiting, said, 'oh no take that off!' She then gifted me with a brand-new dress.

Many of us as Christians are walking around in our tight dresses convincing ourselves we didn't gain the weight. As I read James 1:22, I began to ask myself if I was deceiving myself. James says if I am hearing what God says and not doing it then I am deceiving myself. I am deceiving myself when I think that because I am His child, He will bless my disobedience or somehow understand.

What has God been speaking to you about? Maybe He is speaking to you about unforgiveness or being unequally yoked. Maybe He promised you provision yet you worry to no end because you cannot see how or when or maybe it is some ministry he has spoken into your heart.

Whatever he has spoken that you have not done is disobedience. No matter how we try to justify our disobedience James says we are deceiving ourselves. Today like Paul, I encourage you to check yourself less by believing your justification and lies you are falling when you think you are standing.

Prayer: Lord, today I ask you to search my heart and life for every act of disobedience. Lord, I do not want to deceive myself as to my position or standing with you. Lord, help me not only to hear Your words but to do it also. In Jesus Name.

DAY 26

Remove & Replace

2 Corinthians 10:5 a

Often when we think of demons we think of deliverance services or persons manifesting in a service. What about those thoughts? Those things that only exist in our minds? Those recurring thoughts of self-doubt and fear. Thoughts that tell us we are not loved and we will never succeed no matter how hard we try. The thoughts that tell us about the advice we have for everyone but cannot seem to follow ourselves.

Today Paul reminds us to cast down those thoughts. Throw them down because they go against what God says and they keep us captive. As they circle our minds and hold us hostage our family, our church or even our world waits to experience the best of us. Casting down requires courage and effort on our part. Casting down is difficult but is required. May we make a decision today to cast down those thoughts, cast down doubt, low self-esteem or self-worth, hurt, hate and fear and replace them with what God says about us.

Prayer: Lord, today I admit that there are some thoughts that run through my mind that do not line up with your word. Father many of these thoughts shape my action or inaction. Today, I ask you to purge my mind with the hyssop of your word so that I can regain focus and position myself for my destiny in you. In Jesus Name.

DAY 27

Partial Obedience is still full Disobedience

Key Verse: Joshua 7:1

On the heels of winning one of the most amazing battles where they didn't have to lift a finger, Israel found itself squarely in the anger of God. Why? In the sixth chapter, Joshua gave two instructions: Don't shout until I tell you and Stay away from the devoted things so that you do not bring your own destruction.

The entire team did well in marching around the city once a day with their mouth closed for six days. On the seventh day they marched around seven times but the devoted things called Achan's name. Achan obeyed partially but his partial obedience put him in the seat of God's anger. Maybe Achan was materialistic, greedy or maybe he thought that he could use these things to help the people. Whatever good reason he told himself to justify his actions God was angry. What about you?

Maybe you are dating an unsaved person but not having sex with them. This is partial obedience but in God's sight it is still full disobedience. Maybe you have only been giving a portion or none of your tithes but you come to church faithfully. Again, this partial obedience is full disobedience. Maybe you have not been committing to regular devotion and prayer. This too is partial obedience but to God it is still full disobedience. Maybe you believe you have forgiven but you are still holding the person for ransom. Whatever it is today if you are not carrying out the full instruction it is still disobedience.

Disobedience is sin and sin equals death and hell. Today, I ask God to help us to be totally obedient because with all that we do if we partially obey we can still very well find ourselves in hell.

Prayer: Lord, I am often tempted to take matters into my own hands. Sometimes I do not carry out your commands or instructions fully and I try to appease myself with the thought that I tried. Father, help me to always remember that partial obedience is still full disobedience and that you require total Obedience. In Jesus Name.

DAY 28

Show me the locust

Key Verse: Joel 1:5

In Joel 1:2-4 we see how the locust destroyed all the food of Judah. Every good tree was stripped down to its bark. No trees meant no food, no fruits and no vegetables. Somehow the people of Judah managed to sleep through this ordeal and needed the prophet Joel to awaken them.

It seems a little unreal that they could sleep through a famine? This situation prompted the thought that there might be locusts in my life eating away while I sleep. My next thought was for God to show me the locusts.

As believers there are locusts around us eating away at our peace through issues on our job, in our homes and even in our churches. There are locusts of busyness, laziness and tiredness eating away at our devotional times. There are locusts of anger and malice eating away at our joy. There are locusts of immorality eating away at our purity. There are locusts of greed and materialism eating away at our church time. There are locusts of fear eating away at our faith. There are locusts of pride eating away at our humility and damaging relationships and people in our path.

Some of us are intentionally asleep because we do not want the drama of confrontation while some of us fell asleep unaware. Wherever you are, if there are locusts eating away at your spiritual life it is only a matter of time before you begin to experience a famine if you haven't already. I encourage you to wake up and ask God to show you the locusts in your life!

Prayer: Lord, I thank You that You always have a man in the gap ready to sound the alarm. Father today I lay my life before You asking You to expose the locusts and when you have revealed them grant me the strength to deal with them in Jesus name.

DAY 29

Joy Assassins

Key Verse: Joel 1:16

There is this lady I know who was absolutely bubbly, joyous and joyful. One day in what seemed like a blink of an eye her smile turned into a frown. She began to lose weight and eventually she became depressed. Something or someone had taken her joy.

There are many things in life that come to steal our joy. In the case of Judah a famine swept through their land and hunger killed their joy. What's killing your joy? The lady above was under severe financial burdens that killed her joy. Is loneliness killing your joy?

The truth is sometimes we can be in a crowd and still feel alone. Did you think the dream guy would have been here already and God is delaying so long that there seems to be a man famine? Is sickness killing your joy? Have you been suffering for so long with no end in sight? Is busyness killing your joy? Are there so many demands from so many people but not enough of you to go around? Do you have enough time for God or yourself? Maybe disappointment is killing your joy. You thought that God would have stepped into your situation by now but it seems like the devil has you in cycles or circles.

Whatever your situation be reminded that the joy of the Lord is our strength. If we allow anything to kill our joy we are as good as dead because we will not have the strength to fight. In God's presence there is fullness of joy. Do not allow circumstances to pull you out of his presence because that is where your strength is.

Prayer: Lord, there are so many circumstances in life that threaten to pull me out of your presence and rob me of Your joy. Today I ask that you will help me to remain focused on You and stay in Your presence. Help me to not let anything or anyone draw me away from your presence. In Jesus Name.

DAY 30

The Candle in the Sunlight

Key Verse: Phillipians 3:8

Paul says I count all that I have accomplished dung so that I may get into God and He (God) can get into me.

As I thought about this I thought this might be easy for someone who hasn't accomplished much. However, if you have a husband, children, a house, a career, a degree, a car (add your accomplishments) all of which you worked hard for, counting all of it garbage might be hard. First off the people in this scenario would be offended that they are considered garbage and we would not be able to bring ourselves to downplay the things we have worked so hard to accomplish.

However Paul, who was accomplished in his own right, says all of it is garbage. Everything that we have accomplished pale in comparison to who God is and what He can do. Our efforts are like a candle in the sunlight compared to who God is. So why is it so hard to let go of the candle for the sunlight?

For many of us, who we are is wrapped up in what we have done or accomplished. For others their identities have been built on accomplishments and not on God. True identity comes from God. Anything else is a moving target that keeps us in a cycle of failure and disappointments.

Today I pray God gives us the strength to let go of who we think we are so that we can embrace who God says we are. Out your candle today so that you can appreciate the morning light.

Prayer: Lord, I admit today that I am still trying to hold on to the person that I think I am. I pray God that I will let go of my thoughts of me and grab hold of the thoughts You think towards me. Lord help me to lose myself and find who I should be in You. In Jesus Name.

DAY 31

Do not Grow Weary

Key Verse: Hebrews 12:3-4

There are so many people and things vying for our attention and our affection.

Sometimes all of the demands can leave us drained and weary and wanting to give up. On this Christian journey I have encountered countless situations that made me want to quit. However, Hebrews reminds us to look at Jesus. In spite of being mocked and beaten, in spite of the insults hurled at him and having spit in his face Jesus endured the cross for you and me. Hebrews reminds us that whatever we are facing we haven't had to shed our blood.

It doesn't matter what our situations look like. One thing is certain, our God is faithful. May we never forget in this world of unfaithfulness that one thing holds true. God is faithful no matter what. He is faithful when we are sure about Him and even when we doubt. He is faithful when we fear and when we have faith. He is faithful when we can feel Him near and faithful when He seems so far away. God is faithful when I am faithless. Our God is faithful no matter what!

Look at the example of Jesus and be encouraged. Don't grow weary. We will reap if we faint not.

Prayer: Lord, I thank you that this Christian race is not for the fit but for he that endures to the end. Father, help me to not grow weary. Father, help me to always remember that You are forever faithful and that Your Son endured much at the cross for me. In Jesus name Amen.

COMMITMENTS

Printed in the United States
By Bookmasters